IN THEIR OWN WORDS

SPIES AND CODE BREAKERS

A Primary Source History

Carey Scott

Gareth Stevens
Publishing

KEY TO SYMBOLS
The following symbols highlight the sources of material from the past.

FILM EXCERPT *Primary source material from a film about the subject matter.*

SONG/POEM *Text from songs or poems about the subject matter.*

OFFICIAL SPEECH *Transcribed words from official government speeches.*

GOVERNMENT DOCUMENT *Text extracted from an official government document.*

LETTER *Text from a letter written by a participant in the events.*

PLAQUE/INSCRIPTION *Text taken from plaques or monuments erected in memory of events described in this book.*

INTERVIEW/BOOK EXTRACT *Text from an interview or book.*

NEWSPAPER ARTICLE *Extracts from newspapers of the period.*

TELEGRAM *Text from a telegram sent to or by a participant in the events.*

Cover photos:

Top left: The Enigma decoding machine used during World War II is being inspected by code breaker Ryszard Dembinski.

Top right: Detail from a letter that discusses ex-CIA agent Aldrich Ames who became a Soviet spy during the Cold War.

Background: Modern spy satellites high above Earth monitor human activities on the ground.

CONTENTS

Above: *Spies have always used gadgets to help them carry out espionage. This watch with a hidden camera was made in 1886.*

S pies and code breakers have been around as long as there have been secrets to uncover and codes to crack. Every government uses spying, or espionage, to learn about developments in other nations. Both espionage and code breaking helped the Allied nations win World War II (1939–1945). Espionage was also the most important weapon of the Cold War, the nonmilitary arms race between the United States and the Soviet Union.

INTELLIGENCE AGENCIES

Most espionage is conducted by spies working for government agencies, such as the Central Intelligence Agency (CIA). Governments use intelligence agencies to learn facts about foreign countries that they could not otherwise uncover. They may also use those agencies to spy on people in their own countries. Most countries have one organization for gathering intelligence at home (in Britain MI5, in the United States the FBI) and another for working abroad (MI6 and CIA, respectively). Those organizations also carry out counterintelligence—self-protection against spying by enemy nations. Most governments use espionage against friendly nations as well as hostile ones. Intelligence gained from spying can give a nation advantages at the negotiating table and in business. In wartime, governments use espionage to gain military advantages.

MILITARY SECRETS

Military secrets often reveal technical information about the development of weapons, troop movements, or the locations of weapons' factories. In wartime, knowing the enemy's troop movements can give a massive advantage to a country, but military secrets are important in peacetime, too. During the Cold War, both the United States and the Soviet Union were anxious to know the number, size, and range of the other's nuclear weapons. That knowledge gave both countries advantages in the event of a real war.

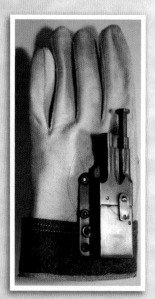

Above: *A pistol glove issued by the U.S. Navy during World War II gave a spy the advantage of being armed while keeping both hands free.*

POLITICAL SECRETS

Awareness of another country's political secrets can be an advantage in international relations. If a government knows about the political or trade alliances or treaties another nation is establishing, that government can plan a more effective strategy.

ECONOMIC SECRETS

Economic secrets are among the information that is most commonly sought. That information may give technical facts about new inventions or advancements in weapons technologies. Advancements in communications technology, for example, or advancements in genetics, can be highly valuable. Being able to capitalize on another country's technology can help build wealth. If a new invention has a military use it can benefit that country's security, too.

Above: *Satellite dishes can be used to intercept e-mail and phone communication. Some people argue that there is too much surveillance in modern societies.*

WHO THEY ARE

A professional spy is sometimes called an intelligence officer, or agent. He or she is a highly trained member of an intelligence agency. He or she may work openly or covertly—under the cover of a false occupation, such as a political diplomat. Intelligence officers gather information, and employ nonprofessional spies for the same task. In this role, agents are sometimes called handlers. They are likely to be people whose jobs give them access to secret information. Handlers and other spies are motivated by money or because of their beliefs. An effective intelligence officer may have a whole network of handlers.

Above: *This WWII map of German-occupied territory was hidden inside a playing card.*

TAPS AND BUGS

Spies collect information by recording conversations and copying secret documents.

Right: *The headquarters of the Central Intelligence Agency is located in Langley, Virginia.*

Above: *The Watergate Hotel was the scene of the break-in and wire-tapping scandal that led to the forced resignation of U.S. President Richard Nixon in 1974.*

Above: *This ballpoint pen has been stripped away to show the tiny radio transmitter inside it.*

Cold War spies used miniature cameras, some so tiny that they were disguised as coat buttons, to photograph documents. Telephone taps and "bugs" (tiny, concealed microphones) were widely used in the 1960s. Soviet Secret Service or KGB officers were known to have bribed hotel staff to plant bugs inside the shoes of visiting Western diplomats. Miniature transmitters, microphones, and batteries transformed targets into walking radio stations, broadcasting their conversations to specific monitoring posts.

CODES AND CIPHERS

Spying also involves sending, intercepting, and interpreting messages. In the early 1900s, individuals created codes or ciphers (messages in symbols) for sending information. Individual code breakers cracked, or solved, those messages. That method changed around 1917 when the first cipher machine was invented. It automatically encrypted the text typed on its keyboard, converting plaintext into "code" or "cipher" text. The recipients of the message set their machine up in the same way as the sender's to convert the message back to readable text.

By 1939, the military on both sides of World War II used cipher machines to encrypt their messages. The governments of the warring nations urgently wanted to read each other's messages to learn their military plans. But it was impossible for individual code breakers to crack the machine-made ciphers. So, Britain and the United States assembled teams of mathematicians. Those teams designed machines that could carry out the millions of calculations needed to read the messages. Code-breaking machines were the forerunners of today's computers. Now, people with coding skills work with computers as programmers—code makers— or illegally as hackers—code breakers. The Internet has changed the role of the spy as well as the code breaker. Often, spies can access information on the Internet. They can also use code breaking skills to hack into protected computer networks to steal secret information.

DIGITAL SPYING

Today's digital technology has enabled modern spies to steal information more easily and more effectively than ever before. Modern spies may choose from a huge range of digital tools disguised as everyday objects. In some cases, the technology has even taken over altogether. Satellites hover above Earth, observing events in such detail they can even photograph and transmit the headlines on a newspaper. The same satellites can capture telephone and computer data and relay it to ground stations for immediate computer analysis.

Today's digital satellites are far more advanced than the military satellites first launched in the 1960s. Modern digital satellites relay information in seconds. Early satellites faced the challenge of retrieving

the film from the cameras within the satellite. The operators ejected the (undeveloped) film toward Earth in a small container. When the container entered the upper atmosphere, a parachute deployed to slow its progress. The film was then caught in mid-air by an airplane and sent to its expected point of entry. That difficult feat was remarkably successful most of the time, and continued to be used until 1972.

Above: *Spy satellites are valuable tools for military intelligence gathering. As they orbit Earth, they photograph different countries' military installations.*

Below: *Between 2001 and 2002 British hacker Gary McKinnon (1966–) hacked into dozens of U.S. Army computers, as well as 16 NASA computers. He claims to have been looking for information on UFOs. In 2008, McKinnon was sentenced to one year in U.S. prison.*

Right: *Matt Damon plays ex-CIA agent Jason Bourne in* The Bourne Identity. *Films like this one and the* Mission: Impossible *series have created an interest in modern spies.*

World War II was a global conflict in which most of the world's nations were united in their cause to fight Japan, Germany, and Italy, a group known as the Axis powers. The opponents, led by Britain, the United States, and the Soviet Union, were the Allied nations. As the Allied and Axis powers fought each other, a secret or "shadow" war was being fought by each nations's spies.

SOLDIERS OF A SHADOW WAR

Some World War II spies worked for both the Allied and Axis nations. Those spies were called double agents. The agents who worked for both sides often supported resistance fighters. Members of the resistance were citizens who fought independently against enemy forces occupying their homeland. Double agents were often able to obtain the enemy's military secrets. They could then spread incorrect information in order to mislead the enemy.

SCHOOLS FOR SPIES

In 1940, British Prime Minister Winston Churchill established an organization to recruit and train secret agents. It was called the Special Operations Executive (SOE). Two years later a similar organization, the Office of Strategic Services (OSS), was established in the United States. By 1944, those two organizations controlled a secret army of more than 20,000 spies. Unlike the military, that shadow army was made up of unconventional individuals. Spies were familiar with an occupied country and fluent in its language. Spies came from all backgrounds: professional athletes, artists and writers, and even convicted criminals. Famous female spies included a circus acrobat and a princess from India.

"We must use many different methods, including military sabotage, labor agitations and strikes, continuous propaganda, terrorist acts against traitors and German leaders, boycotts, and riots."

Hugh Dalton (1887–1962), the first boss of the SOE, who trained British spies during World War II

Right: *Soviet Premier Joseph Stalin (1879–1953, left), U.S. President Franklin D. Roosevelt (1882–1945, center), and British Prime Minister Winston Churchill (1874–1965) met at the Teheran Conference in Persia (Iran) during World War II.*

CAMP X

At SOE training schools in Britain, and a "university of espionage" called Camp X in Canada, would-be spies learned the techniques of guerrilla warfare. That is a type of combat that takes place in settings that are familiar to local fighters, but are challenging for conventional armies, such as rural, urban, or mountainous terrains. Candidates were taught how to kill silently, use ciphers and Morse code, and employ methods of sabotage. At Camp X, students underwent a series of rigorous tests. Those tests often ended in real missions, such as planting fake explosives. If an agent was caught, the OSS would not help him. He would be interrogated and beaten by the FBI to determine whether he would reveal his identity. At the end of the course, new recruits were invited to a party. But even that celebration was a test to see if they would reveal their cover under the influence of alcohol.

Above: *Resistance saboteurs from Europe and the United States used demolition charges like this to set off explosions. The firing device is on the left.*

THE RIGHT EQUIPMENT

Once agents had "graduated," they were supplied with everything they needed to operate as spies. They were provided with expertly forged passports, identity and ration cards, driving licenses, and work permits. Axis counterespionage experts paid close attention to details. They could often tell where a suit was made from how it was tailored. To help protect the spies' identity, local clothing was obtained whenever possible. Dental work was sometimes redone to look as though a local dentist had carried it out. Agents needed to defend themselves as well as to fit in, so they were equipped with specially concealed weapons,

TIME LINE
1918-1939

1918
Enigma cipher machine is patented by a German businessman, who begins selling it to banks and businesses.

1920
William F. Friedman (1891–1969) coins the term "cryptanalysis" to describe code breaking.

1926
The Enigma machine is bought by the Germans to secure their communications.

1930
Signals Intelligence Service (SIS) is established as the code breaking division of the U.S. Army.

1932
A team of mathematicians at the Polish Cipher Bureau solves the Enigma code.

1939
Poland gives British Intelligence valuable material on Enigma.

> "What they teach you at sabotage school will blow your mind. Six or seven people that are properly trained can cripple a good-sized city. It is as easy as can be. We learned how to operate and destroy locomotives and power plants, communications systems, and telephones … we were taught how to fight dirty."
>
> **Frank Gleason, Office of Strategic Services (OSS) recruit, 1941**

such as the "Stinger," a tiny gun disguised as a pen, or a deadly blade inside the heel of a shoe. Commonly, one coat button was actually a suicide pill. A number of captured agents bit down on those deadly buttons to avoid interrogation after being caught.

ESPIONAGE SUCCESSES

British spies, working for the SOE, operated in all the countries occupied by Nazi Germany. The biggest SOE group was in France, where the resistance movement was strongest. While British spies were mostly concerned with supporting the resistance with acts of sabotage, agents working for the United States were more concerned with gathering intelligence.

Future CIA leader Allen Dulles recruited one of the most successful spies of the war to work for the United States. In 1942, Dulles was assigned to Berne, Switzerland, to gather German intelligence. Switzerland was a neutral country surrounded by Axis nations, making it an ideal and dangerous base. In Berne, a German diplomat named Fritz Kolbe offered to spy for the British, but SOE leaders suspected him of being a double agent and rejected him. Kolbe then approached Dulles, who had Kolbe's background vetted, or checked, by counterintelligence before taking him on.

Kolbe was motivated purely by a hatred of Nazism. He refused any payment, and often put himself at great risk to obtain information useful to the Allied powers. Over the next two years, Kolbe passed more than 2,000 documents detailing Nazi secrets to Dulles. One of the problems facing Dulles was how to transport secret maps, drawings, and reports out of Switzerland. Kolbe had to travel through enemy territory to the OSS headquarters in Algiers, North Africa. Kolbe devised a complicated courier system that took 10 to 12 days. In Berne, the documents were photographed onto microfilm, and the film was given to the driver of a train headed for Lyon, France. The driver hid the microfilm in a secret compartment near the engine. On arrival in Lyon, the driver passed the microfilm to an OSS agent, who bicycled it to Marseille, in the south of France. From there it was transported to the French

"You have been given a cover story and papers in the name of Yves Le Bras, which you will use for your normal life in the field. To cover your personality as an agent, use the name Bastien.

You will receive and send messages for Elie's circuit. You will send only those messages which are passed to you by Elie or which are approved by him. . . . The circuit password of Elie and Paul is:

'I come on behalf of Celestin. Ah, yes, the wine merchant.'

You will sever your contact with the people who receive you as soon as possible and, after that, will refrain from contacting members of any circuit apart from your own.

Regarding your wireless communication with us, we would stress that you should only be on the air when necessary and that your transmissions should be as short as possible."

An excerpt from a set of orders for an SOE spy about to enter German-occupied France

Right: *The United States tested the V-2 rocket in New Mexico, in the late 1940s. V-2s were fired at European cities during World War II.*

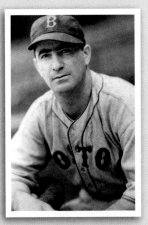

"Following his 15-year career with five different major league teams, the Princeton-educated Moe Berg served as a highly successful Office of Strategic Services (OSS) operative during World War II. Among his many missions on behalf of OSS, the former catcher was charged with learning all he could about Hitler's nuclear bomb project.

Because of his intellect, Berg is considered the 'brainiest' man ever to have played the game. He spoke a dozen languages fluently and often autographed pictures in Japanese."

From a CIA Exhibit in Langley, Virginia, honoring WW II spy Moe Berg (1902–1972), a former Major League catcher

TIME LINE 1939–1940

JUNE 1939
Bletchley Park, near London, becomes the British center for intelligence.

SEPTEMBER 1939
Britain and France declare war on Germany after the Nazis invade Poland.

MAY 1940
The Twenty Committee begins running Operation Double Cross in Britain.

MARCH 1940
Alan Turing produces the Bombe, a decoding machine.

JULY 1940
The Special Operations Executive (SOE) is formed by Winston Churchill in Britain.

island of Corsica by ship, and then to Algiers by plane. Kolbe was never discovered. His intelligence warned the Allies that a German agent was working in the British ambassador's home in Turkey. He reported on the development of the V-1 and V-2 rockets that rained down on London in the last days of World War II. Kolbe also described Japanese military plans in Southeast Asia.

OPERATION DOUBLE CROSS

At the start of the war, the British intelligence agency MI5 created a plan called Operation Double Cross. In 1939, Germany began parachuting spies into Britain in an attempt to gather intelligence for an invasion (Operation Sealion) which was never put into action. Compared to British spies placed in enemy territory, most German agents were woefully unprepared. They had little training, spoke poor English, and their documents were clumsily forged. Most German spies were easily spotted, and others gave themselves up. In all, 138 German

Above: *German Axis troops march into Allied Poland.*

"My aim was to help shorten the war for my unfortunate countrymen and to help concentration camp inmates avoid further suffering."

Fritz Kolbe, in a letter written from Switzerland, 1965

Above: *Allied air force planes drop supplies to agents waiting in German-occupied Holland.*

GERMANY HONORS THE "TRAITOR" SPY WHO GAVE NAZI SECRETS TO AMERICA

"Kolbe was described by the CIA as the most important spy of [World War II]. As a bureaucrat in Adolf Hitler's foreign ministry, he smuggled 2,600 secret Nazi documents to American intelligence in Switzerland from 1943 onwards, continuing his task undetected until the war ended. Yet after the war, Kolbe was dismissed as a traitor by successive German governments. His attempts to rejoin the foreign ministry were repeatedly rejected and he was forced to end his days working as a salesman for an American chainsaw company, until his death in Switzerland in 1971."

Excerpt from *The Independent*, September 25, 2004

agents landed and were captured on Britain's shores. Some Germans were executed, others imprisoned, but 40 of them were persuaded to become double agents for the M15. They transmitted false intelligence back to Germany—Operation Double Cross—a calculated mixture of facts and misinformation. The British MI5 misled the German Intelligence organization, the Abwehr, for the rest of the World War II.

THE MAKING OF A SUPERSPY

The M15 groomed one of its agents, Danish-born Wulf Schmidt (1912–1992, codename "Tate") as a superspy. The M15 created a false network of spies for Schmidt. That gave the appearance that he was able to collect intelligence on many topics. He led the Nazis to believe that they controlled a successful spy ring in Britain; they added agents to the ring—straight into the hands of the MI5. In 1944, German handlers asked their British agents for reports on the landing sites of their deadly V-2 rockets, and Schmidt and his colleagues sent back false reports

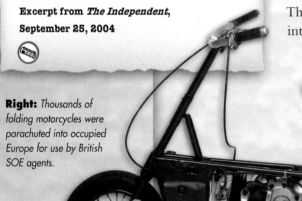

Right: *Thousands of folding motorcycles were parachuted into occupied Europe for use by British SOE agents.*

Above: *London was bombed during the Blitz in World War II. More than 20,000 people were killed, and a million homes were damaged. Without Operation Double Cross, however, the damage may have been worse.*

TIME LINE
1940–1941

OCTOBER 1940
The German Air Force fails to destroy the British Royal Air Force in the Battle of Britain.

DECEMBER 1940
U.S. code breakers, led by William F. Friedman, break Purple, Japan's secret code.

MAY 1941
British Royal Navy officers capture an Enigma machine and codebooks from a German U-Boat.

that indicated the rockets weren't reaching their targets. Using the false information, the Germans adjusted the rockets' range. After, V–2s missed the center of London. The Nazis were often misled by Schmidt and others. Toward the end of the war, the Nazi government actually awarded some double agents—including Schmidt—with Germany's highest military honor: the Iron Cross.

THE ABWEHR IN AMERICA

German espionage in Britain and in the United States was a dismal failure. In the 1930s, the Abwehr had a network of more than 30 agents working in the United States. Most were German-born Americans who passed the organization information about U.S. technology and national defense. But in 1939, the Abwehr made a mistake when it tried to blackmail William Sebold into becoming the ring's radio operator. Sebold, a loyal U.S. citizen, went straight to the FBI and became a double agent. For 16 months FBI agents watched and filmed German spies passing information to Sebold. The agents also provided false intelligence for Sebold to transmit. After, the FBI closed down Germany's U.S. Abwehr operation and arrested every spy. Germany could no longer access information on U.S. preparations for war, including the development of the technologies that would later defeat the Germans.

SPYING FOR JAPAN

The Japanese attack on Pearl Harbor, Hawaii, pulled the United States into World War II. The December 7, 1941 bombings took Americans

Below: *Admiral Wilhelm Canaris (1887–1945) was head of the Abwehr until 1944.*

by surprise. Japanese Intelligence had been preparing for the attack for a long time, however. As far back as 1935, Japan had recruited a German family to spy for them in Hawaii.

The Kühn family bought a cottage house in Honolulu overlooking the harbor. Large sums of money regularly appeared in the Kühn family bank account, although Dr. Bernard Kühn was unemployed. Each one of the Kühns played a role in the family spy ring. Mother Friedel and daughter Ruth operated a beauty salon where most of their customers were the wives of high-ranking naval officers. Attractive, outgoing Ruth dated American sailors, eventually becoming engaged to a young officer. Dr. Kühn and Friedel took walks in the mountains above Pearl Harbor, and they always had a pair of binoculars with them. They sailed around the harbor in their sailboat, making notes. Dr. Kühn regularly took his ten-year-old son, Eberhard, for walks along the waterfront, and the officers of warships sometimes invited the boy for tours of their vessels. The naval officers thought that the boy was asking questions merely out of curiosity, but the reality was sinister. Eberhard had been trained to ask specific questions, and when he returned, Friedel noted his answers. By 1941, preparations for the attack on Pearl Harbor were coming together.

Right: *This miniature camera allowed a German agent to take photographs while pretending to check his watch.*

Above: *The battleship* West Virginia *burns after the Japanese attack on Pearl Harbor in 1941. More than 3,000 Americans died in the bombing, making the U.S. declaration of war against Japan inevitable.*

Right: *In WWII, an agent's radio was commonly concealed in a suitcase. Discovery by the enemy could mean death for the agent. This example is from the United States.*

JUNE 1941
Nazi Germany invades the Soviet Union, as predicted by U.S. intelligence. The invasion breaks a secret nonaggression pact between the two countries.

AUGUST 1941
The assassination of a German naval cadet is the first violent act of resistance in France.

THE DIPLOMAT SPY

Japanese spy Takeo Yoshikawa (1914–1993) was sent to Hawaii to assist the family. Yoshikawa noted when battleships arrived and left the harbor. He went swimming to assess the water's depth and any underwater obstructions, took boat trips to see if there were protective nets in the water, and observed U.S. patrol planes to learn their schedules. The tireless work carried out by the Kühns and Yoshikawa enabled the Japanese to make their attack on Pearl Harbor as destructive as possible. Soon after the attack, the Kühns were discovered, and all but little Eberhard were imprisoned. Yoshikawa's role was not uncovered immediately, however, so he returned to Japan.

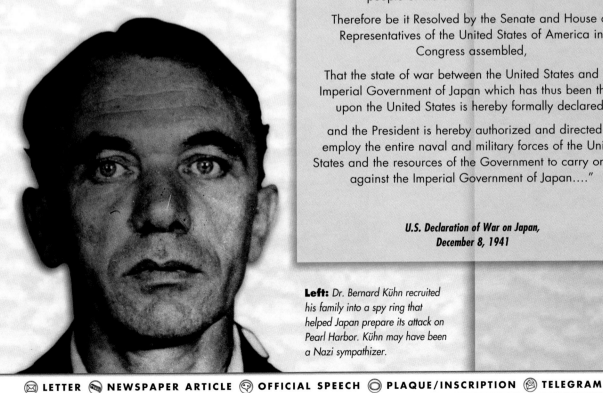

"JOINT RESOLUTION Declaring that a state of war exists between the Imperial Government of Japan and the Government and the people of the United States and making provisions to prosecute the same.

Whereas the Imperial Government of Japan has committed unprovoked acts of war against the Government and the people of the United States of America:

Therefore be it Resolved by the Senate and House of Representatives of the United States of America in Congress assembled,

That the state of war between the United States and the Imperial Government of Japan which has thus been thrust upon the United States is hereby formally declared;

and the President is hereby authorized and directed to employ the entire naval and military forces of the United States and the resources of the Government to carry on war against the Imperial Government of Japan...."

U.S. Declaration of War on Japan, December 8, 1941

Left: *Dr. Bernard Kühn recruited his family into a spy ring that helped Japan prepare its attack on Pearl Harbor. Kühn may have been a Nazi sympathizer.*

Above: *Alan Turing (1912–1954), a mathematical genius, did the most to break the German code Enigma.*

Most messages passed between officials during World War II were sent by radio. They were transmitted in code so they seemed meaningless to eavesdroppers. That was nothing new—codes had been used for centuries to keep information private. But in the 1940s, machines were being used to create complex codes that seemed unbreakable. The science of cryptanalysis was developed to break those machine-made codes.

BLETCHLEY PARK

A British code breaking organization was established in 1939. Government Communications Headquarters (GCHQ) was established outside London in a Victorian mansion called Bletchley Park. Bletchley Park code breakers were given the mission to intercept and break German codes. A huge team of agents was needed for this task. Recruiters searched Britain's universities for mathematics and language experts. A brilliant young mathematician, Alan Turing, was among those students recruited. Recruiters knew that the cryptanalysts were often excellent chess players and puzzle solvers, so they also set up a competition in a daily newspaper in which readers were asked to finish a puzzle in 12 minutes. Those who completed it received a letter inviting them for an interview to become part of the Bletchley Park team.

"No mention whatsoever may be made either in conversation or correspondence regarding the nature of your work. It is expressly forbidden to bring cameras within the precincts of Bletchley Park (Official Secrets Act).

DO NOT TALK AT MEALS. There are waitresses and others who may not be in the know regarding your particular work.

DO NOT TALK WHILE TRAVELING. Indiscretions have been overheard on Bletchley platform.

DO NOT TALK IN THE [SOLDIERS' QUARTERS]. Why expect your hosts who are not pledged to secrecy to be more discreet than you?"

Excerpt from the regulations for Bletchley Park employees

A PERFECT CIPHER MACHINE?

The Germans often used a cipher machine called Enigma to encrypt their messages. In the 1920s, the German military modified Enigma several times, making it increasingly more complicated. By the start of the war, the Nazis were convinced that Enigma was secure. Enigma used three rotors (wheels) and a plugboard to encrypt

Above: *Bletchley Park became the center for British code breaking during World War II. It is now a museum.*

messages. When a letter was typed by keyboard, a rotor automatically substituted another letter for it. When that same letter was typed again, a different letter was substituted for it. After 26 letters had been typed, the first rotor returned to its starting place and the second rotor began to operate, one letter at a time. Each rotor was wired differently so that it produced different substitutions.

> "At least half of the people there were absolutely mad. They were geniuses, no doubt many of them were extremely, extremely clever, but my goodness they were strange in ordinary life."
>
> **Gwen Davies, Bletchley Park employee, remembers codebreakers' eccentricity**

The plugboard, which contained wiring and jacks, or plugs, provided yet another level of encryption by swapping letters again. The plugboard and rotors could be set to different positions, changing the ciphers once more. Operators re-set them, sometimes daily, to positions that were set out in military codebooks. To read an Enigma message, an operator needed an identical machine set to the same positions. Enigma used more than a million symbols before it repeated one. It seemed secure, but the Germans did not allow for theft or human error.

BREAKING ENIGMA

The most significant codebreaking theft was carried out before the war by Hans-Thilo Schmidt, a Polish spy and an employee of Germany's Cipher Office. In the 1920s, the Polish government had begun an intelligence gathering operation to discover Nazi military goals. A team of young mathematicians, led by Marian Rejewski, was recruited in 1932 to break the Enigma code. In a stroke of luck, Rejewski was given operating instructions and lists

TIME LINE 1941–1942

OCTOBER 1941
Intelligence enables Allied forces to sink five ships headed to Nazi General Rommel's African campaign.

DECEMBER 1941
Japanese attack on Pearl Harbor, Hawaii, brings the United States into WWII; Camp X opens in Ontario, Canada.

MAY 1942
Navajo recruits develop a code based on their language.

> "I must make provisions for being captured... The manner of my writing will give you the following information.
>
> 'My dearest Mother' = Confidential books destroyed.
>
> 'Best Love, Godfrey' = Sunk by depth charges.
>
> 'Love, Godfrey' = Sunk by mine on surface.
>
> 'Best love from your loving son, Godfrey' = Sunk by torpedo on surface.
>
> 'Love from your loving son, Godfrey' = Rammed.
>
> Keep this locked away and keep it to yourselves please."
>
> **A secret code created by a British Royal Navy Lieutenant to communicate with his superiors**

Left: A scene from the film Enigma (2001), which told the story of breaking of the German code at Bletchley Park.

Above: *Nazi leader Reinhard Heydrich (1904–1942) was assassinated by SOE agents.*

Below: *This statue of mathematician and code breaker Marian Rejewski (1905–1980) was erected in Bydgoszcz, Poland.*

of Enigma settings by Schmidt. Those documents enabled Rejewski to build a replica Enigma called Bomba. By 1938, Polish Intelligence was reading about 75 percent of Germany's secret messages.

THE BOMBE

In 1939, with the Nazis poised to invade Poland, Polish Intelligence revealed everything they knew about Enigma to their British counterparts. With that help from the Polish team, Bletchley Park agent and mathematician Alan Turing produced an improved version of Rejewski's Bomba. Turning called his machine Bombe. To decode messages, code breakers had to find a "crib"—a bit of encrypted text that they could translate. A crib was usually created from repeated words or phrases. The trick was finding chunks of phrasing that repeated from message to message. Luckily for the code breakers, the Nazi operators often ended their messages patriotically with "Heil Hitler." Another repeatedly used phrase was "Nothing to report." When code breakers recognized those repeated phrases, they had the clues they needed to break larger chunks of information. Those repeated phrases were the human error that helped break Enigma.

Above: *The invasion into Poland by Nazi forces in 1939 launched Europe into WWII and created a demand for code breaking.*

ULTRA INTELLIGENCE

Enigma codebooks, which typically showed one month's plugboard and rotor settings, were so valuable that secret operations were carried out to steal them. The most successful of those secret tasks was Operation Primrose, in which a number of codebooks and an Enigma machine were recovered from a bombed U-boat in 1941. By 1945, there were more than 200 Bombes in operation. By the end of World War II, most Enigma messages transmitted by the German armed forces and Abwehr were being read by Allied forces. That intelligence was called Ultra. It was an important part of the Allied victory in the Battle of the Atlantic—the German attempt to sink Britain's supply ships. Ultra also helped British Intelligence learn if the misinformation transmitted through double agents was being taken seriously by the enemy.

> "We worked with brilliant linguists from Oxford and Cambridge. When we received the German messages which had been decoded, they translated them from German into English, and then sent those to typists to be typed up. Then they were brought back, and we had to check them very carefully, with the handwritten translations, so that there were no typing errors. Those decoded messages gave the positions of the U-boats out in the Atlantic, and so you can imagine that a number 3 altered to a number 5, and a number 6 altered to a number 8 could have fatal consequences...."
>
> **Diane Neal, a Bletchley Park employee**

PURPLE AND THE MAGICIANS

In 1939, Japanese Intelligence devised a more effective cipher machine than Enigma, which Americans called Purple. Although the United States had not yet joined the war, the U.S. Army's Signal Intelligence Service (SIS) was given the task of breaking Purple. The head of the SIS was a brilliant code breaker named William F. Friedman. Everyone on his 12-person team was a mathematical genius referred to as a "magician." Under Friedman's leadership, mathematicians worked compulsively, even solving ciphers in their spare time. Friedman and his wife, who was also a devoted and accomplished code breaker, held dinner parties for the team. In order to attend, code breakers had to solve a cipher informing them of the name of the restaurant and its address. The team also sent each other Christmas and birthday cards in cipher, competing with one another to devise the most difficult puzzles.

Friedman and his group began studying intercepted Purple messages. They hoped that a mathematical analysis would give them clues about the type of cipher machine that had created them. Not only did they have to work with the complex Japanese language, they also had no idea what type of cipher machine was used to create the codes. Friedman and his team looked for cribs, and soon discovered that the Japanese

Right: *The Enigma cipher machine looked much like a typewriter with extra features—a plugboard and rotors to encrypt messages.*

TIME LINE
1942–1945

MAY 1942
Reinhard Heydrich, chief of Reich Security for the Nazis, is assassinated by SOE agents.

JULY 1942
U.S. President Roosevelt establishes the U.S. Office of Strategic Services (OSS).

SEPTEMBER 1944
V-2 rockets hit London, but Operation Double Cross minimizes damage to the city.
Four female SOE agents are executed at a Nazi concentration camp.

MARCH 1945
The United States captures Iwo Jima.

MAY 1945
Germany surrenders, ending World War II.

Above: *Cryptanalyst Elizebeth Friedman (1892–1980) introduced her husband William to cryptology.*

"A cipher is different from a code. . . . In code systems, the units or symbols to be translated can be of different lengths: a letter, a syllable, a word, a sentence, or just a string of letters or numbers is agreed to stand for a particular word or a whole phrase in the message (for example, 'A cat may look at a King' might be agreed to mean 'Oil shares steady'. . .). In contrast, the units in cipher systems are of uniform length and bear a uniform relationship to the units of the plaintext. Usually one letter in the cipher corresponds to one letter in the message, though in some systems groups of two or even three letters are used in a cipher to stand for one letter in the message."

**William F. and Elizebeth Friedman explain codes and ciphers in their book
The Shakespearian Ciphers Examined**

operators numbered their messages and spelled out the encrypted number at the beginning of each one. A year of intense work followed. Finally, the breakthrough came in 1940. Genevieve Grotjan found a pattern of relationships between ciphertext and plaintext. The team was overjoyed.

By plotting the patterns in the text, the team worked out how Purple operated. Leo Rosen, a former MIT electronics student, was able to build a replica Purple from the team's calculations. Rosen and a colleague finished wiring the machine late one evening, and immediately fed it with a Purple ciphertext message. The plaintext was revealed. Purple was finally broken.

Right: *Operatives work at Colossus, an early computer used at Bletchley Park.*

MAGIC INTELLIGENCE

By autumn 1940, Purple messages were being decrypted. The intelligence gained from Purple was often called Magic, in honor of the mathematicians. Only Japan's diplomats used Purple machines—the Japanese armed forces used different cipher machines. Military messages could not yet be read, but Magic was still a rich source of information. The pro-Nazi Japanese ambassador to Germany frequently had revealing conversations with Hitler. U.S. Intelligence learned that the Nazis planned to invade the Soviet Union. That information was passed to Soviet leader Joseph Stalin, though he did not believe it. At the end of the war, Magic revealed that Japan would not surrender even if it was threatened by invasion. It was that information that led to the dropping of atomic bombs on Hiroshima and Nagasaki in Japan.

Above: This "Purple" cipher machine was used by Japanese diplomats. Two similar Japanese machines were known by the names "Coral" and "Jade."

CODE TALKERS

Friedman's team was responsible for creating codes as well as breaking them. They devised a cipher machine called Sigaba that was used by the

TIME LINE 1945–1948

AUGUST 1945
Atomic bombs are dropped on Hiroshima and Nagasaki, Japan, after intelligence reveals that Japanese surrender is unlikely.

SEPTEMBER 1947
The Central Intelligence Agency (CIA) is established in the United States.

FEBRUARY 1948
The Soviet Union initiates a communist takeover of Czechoslovakia.

JUNE 1948
The Blockade of Berlin begins with the Soviets controlling access to Western-occupied areas of the city.

"ARTICLE 1. Japan recognizes and respects the leadership of Germany and Italy in the establishment of a new order in Europe.

ARTICLE 2. Germany and Italy recognize and respect the leadership of Japan in the establishment of a new order in Greater East Asia.

ARTICLE 3. Japan, Germany, and Italy agree to cooperate in their efforts on aforesaid lines. They further undertake to assist one another with all political, economic, and military means if one of the Contracting Powers is attacked by a Power at present not involved in the European War or in the Japanese-Chinese conflict."

Excerpt from the Tripartite Pact made between Japan, Germany, and Italy, 1940

Left: William F. Friedman headed the team that broke Purple. He became the most famous U.S. code breaker.

Above: *The Sigaba cipher machine, created by the SIS, used more roters than Enigma making it unbreakable.*

U.S. Army and Navy throughout the war. Sigaba was never broken by the enemy, but Sigaba machines were too heavy to be used on the battlefield. Other systems were used for tactical communications. The most successful of those was the code developed by the Navajo code talkers. The code talkers did not need complicated machines. They were able to communicate directly with one another in a verbal code on two-way radios and telephones.

CREATING THE CODE

In 1942, Area Signal Officer Lieutenant Colonel Jones, stationed in San Diego, California, received an intriguing proposal from an engineer, Philip Johnston. Johnston said he could create a secure code for sending and receiving messages on the battlefield.

The son of a missionary, Johnston had grown up on a Navajo reservation in Arizona in the early 1900s. He was one of just 30 non-Navajos who spoke the language. His idea for an unbreakable code was based on the use of the obscure language. There was one hitch, however. There were no Navajo words for many of the military terms that would be needed in battlefield messages. Johnston had a solution. Navajo recruits could create them. Recruiters visited the Navajo reservations in search of suitable candidates. Thirty recruits enlisted in the U.S. Marines. They underwent military and radio operating training and developed the necessary code. The Navajo recruits created a list of more than 200 terms such as "bounded by water," for Britain and "iron hat" for Germany. In the code, a Navajo noun, usually a plant or animal, stood for each letter of the alphabet. Those first recruits were stationed at Guadalcanal in the Solomon Islands. They were immediately successful. A training program was started for more recruits, with Johnston serving as its instructor.

MILITARY TERM	NAVAJO WORD	MEANING
Battleship	Lo-tso	Whale
Aircraft Carrier	Tsidi-ney-ye-hi	Bird carrier
Submarine	Besh-lo	Iron fish
Mine Sweeper	Cha	Beaver
Destroyer	Ca-lo	Shark
Troop Transport	Dinch-nev-ye-hi	Man carrier
Cruiser	Lo-tso-yazzie	Small whale

 Navajo code talkers' terms for ships

VICTORY AT IWO JIMA

The Navajo marines were communications experts and runners (soldiers who delivered messages by hand, often while dodging bullets).

Right: *Former Navajo code talker and U.S. Marine Dan Akee shows the Congressional Medal of Honor awarded to him for bravery during World War II.*

They took part in every battle in the Pacific against Japan. Fighting the Japanese caused them some trouble with their own side, however. Some of the Navajos appeared Asian to U.S. troops. Some Navajos were harassed or even arrested under suspicion of being Japanese spies. One Navajo soldier suspected of spying was assigned a bodyguard after nearly being shot.

Above: In the Pacific, two Navajo code talkers relay orders over the field radio using the Native American language.

At the battle of Iwo Jima, the Navajos were most successful. Throughout the 35-day clash between U.S. and Japanese forces, six code talkers worked around the clock. They sent and received more than 800 messages in the first two days of the battle. After the war, the code talkers' contribution was recognized as vital in the U.S. victory. In all, 420 Navajo code talkers, of which 13 were killed, served in the Marine Corps. The Japanese never broke their code.

APRIL 1949
NATO—a military alliance of 12 nations including the United States and Britain—is established.

OCTOBER 1949
The People's Republic of China is founded by Mao Zedong.

JUNE 1950
The Korean War begins when the Communist North, supported by the Soviet Union, invades the South.

JUNE 1953
Julius and Ethel Rosenberg are executed for treason.

JULY 1953
The Korean War ends.

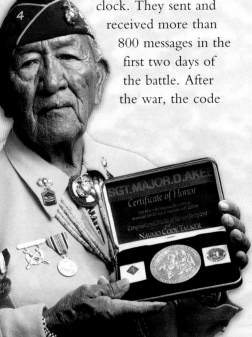

"The conventional code uses numbers and letters and it is scrambled…. And from there it goes to another expert and he unscrambles it. So there's time lost. If a Navajo code-talker is really fluent with his code system he is given a message, it's sent, he looks at it, calls the receiver on the other side, 'Here's the message,' and the receiver will say, 'Go ahead and send it,'… and he encodes them as he is talking and the [other] guy decodes it as he's saying it. It comes through in minutes. Ordinary messages are [delivered in fewer than] three minutes, and when you're doing that, you're saving lives."

Keith Little, Navajo code talker and President of the Navajo Code Talkers Association

Above: *A map shows the countries in the Soviet bloc—nations that were controlled by the Union of Soviet Socialist Republics (U.S.S.R.). Albania split with the U.S.S.R. in the early 1960s, but remained Communist. Although Romania did not split with the U.S.S.R., it maintained a more independent stance than other Soviet bloc countries.*

Below: *Donald Duart Maclean (1913–1983) was a member of the Cambridge Five spy ring.*

From the ashes of World War II, the United States and the Soviet Union—once allies in the fight against the Axis nations—now squared off against one another on the world stage. As the world's two superpowers, they formed alliances with other nations and prepared for battle. The Cold War had begun.

A FIGHT FOR SUPREMACY

The North Atlantic Treaty Organization (NATO) was formed in 1949 as a military alliance between the United States and Western European democracies. That agreement promised U.S. military support if any NATO member country was invaded by a communist nation. The Soviet Union responded with the Warsaw Pact—an alliance between the countries of Eastern Europe that had become communist "satellites" of the Soviet Union following the war. One of those nations was East Germany (which split from Germany in 1949 and became communist). In the Cold War that followed, there was no military conflict. Instead, espionage played a vital role as each country jockeyed for political, economic, and military supremacy—and prepared for battle in case tensions escalated into an actual war.

COMMUNIST PROMISE

Before World War II, when the Soviet Union was still a young nation, communists spoke of building a fair society. In the 1930s, both Britain and the United States had suffered under the Great Depression, an economic crisis that caused massive unemployment and poverty. Communism promised a classless society where wealth would be shared equally between everyone. It was hopes for a fair, classless society that led some people to become spies for the Soviet Union. Among the most famous of those spies were four friends—wealthy

Above: *Britain's Cambridge University was where members of the U.S.S.R.'s top spy ring were educated.*

TIME LINE
1954–1962

Englishmen who had attended Britain's highly regarded Cambridge University. They were Kim Philby (codename "Stanley"), Donald Maclean ("Homer"), Anthony Blunt ("Johnson") and Guy Burgess ("Hicks"). After graduating in the 1930s, all four men gained important posts as government officials. They immediately began passing information to the Soviets during World War II, spying that continued during the Cold War.

MACLEAN'S BRILLIANT CAREER

In 1944, Donald Maclean landed an important post at the British Embassy in Washington, D.C., and he soon became an important spy for the Russians. Maclean attended secret meetings where note taking was forbidden. He memorized the discussions and wrote them up later in the privacy of his home. That information helped Soviet Premier Joseph Stalin plan communist takeovers in Europe.

MARCH 1954
The Soviet Union establishes the KGB.

MAY 1955
The Warsaw Pact, a military alliance between communist states, is formed.

AUGUST 1961
The Berlin Wall is built, preventing travel from East Germany to to the West.

JANUARY 1962
Soviet double agent Kim Philby exposes British secret agent David Cornwell to the KGB.

OCTOBER 1962
The Soviet Union builds missle bases in Cuba, 90 miles (145 km) from Florida.

Left: *Soviet Premier Nikita S. Khrushchev (1894–1971, far left) and U.S. President John F. Kennedy (1917–1963) met during the Cuban Missile Crisis after U.S. spy planes took aerial photos of missile bases in Cuba.*

Below: *Guy Burgess (1911–1963) was a member of the Cambridge Five spy ring.*

"[Philby] carried out his duties ably and conscientiously, and I have no reason to conclude that he has at any time betrayed the interests of his country, or to identify him with the so-called 'Third Man,' if indeed there was one."

British Foreign Secretary Harold Macmillan (1894–1986) in 1955, seven years before Philby was revealed as a spy and the "third man" who tipped off Burgess and Maclean

In 1947, Maclean attended a conference about sharing atomic secrets among Western nations and then shared that information with the Soviet Union. Maclean became such a trusted diplomat that he was given a special pass to visit the U.S. Atomic Energy Commission alone, which even the director of the FBI was not permitted to do. With this pass, Maclean was able to freely rifle through classified files about the development of the nuclear bomb. Because Maclean had a near-photographic memory, he often memorized the contents of documents rather than use the miniature camera given to him to by the Soviets. Every week Maclean went to New York to make a "dead drop"—leaving documents in a prearranged place to be picked up by his handler. He made those trips without ever arousing suspicion because his American wife lived in New York.

PROJECT VENONA

Time ran out for Maclean. In 1946, a top-secret British-U.S. code breaking operation called Project Venona had been set up to decrypt messages sent by the Soviet Union. By 1950, the code names of Soviet spies were becoming known, including Homer, whose messages were sent from New York. Maclean was identified, but the man assigned to discover Homer's identity was none other than Maclean's partner, Kim Philby. He warned Maclean, who immediately deserted Britain, defected to Moscow, and took Guy Burgess, another member of the Cambridge spy ring, with him.

THE ROSENBERGS

Project Venona eventually uncovered the code names of 349 Soviet spies in the United States. Many of them were never be identified. The code names "Liberal" and "Antenna," however, led to a Jewish couple with two children, Julius and Ethel Rosenberg. Information concluded that Julius was running a spy ring for the Soviets and passing classified information from his job in aeronautics. His wife Ethel typed up notes. In 1951, the Rosenbergs were tried in the U.S. court system, found guilty of treason, and sentenced to death. Amid a storm of protest at the harshness of the sentence, the Rosenbergs were executed in 1953.

"Cambridge Spies" Surface in Moscow

"Two British diplomats who vanished in mysterious circumstances five years ago have reappeared in the Soviet Union. Guy Burgess and Donald Maclean handed a statement to the press in a hotel room overlooking Moscow's Red Square. . . .
The former diplomats denied ever having been Soviet agents. They said they had come to the U.S.S.R. to 'work for the aim of better understanding between the Soviet Union and the West.'

In 1951, Guy Burgess and Donald Maclean were recalled to London from the British Embassy in Washington D.C. after confidential documents went missing . . . both men disappeared before they could be questioned.

At the time it was rumored there was a 'third man' who had tipped them off. Since then there has been continuing speculation about a spy ring composed of former Cambridge University students."

From the British Broadcasting Corporation (BBC) Archives, February 11, 1956

Above: *This checkpoint marked a crossing between East and West Berlin. In 1989, after the fall of the Berlin Wall and the unification of Germany, the booth became part of Allied Museum in Berlin, Germany.*

TIME LINE
1963–1967

JANUARY 1963
Kim Philby defects to Moscow just before he is unmasked as a spy.

MARCH 1965
U.S. involvement in the Vietnam War begins.

DECEMBER 1967
John A. Walker (1937–) enters the Soviet Embassy in Washington, D.C., to offer the Russians U.S. military secrets in exchange for quick cash.

Today, most historians agree that the intelligence the Rosenbergs passed to the Soviets was of little value. The same cannot be said for Maclean and his colleagues, none of whom were arrested. Philby provided information that led to the capture and deaths of dozens of British agents. Maclean helped Stalin build the Iron Curtain—the division of Europe into Communist and Democratic states—and advance the Korean War.

SELLING AMERICA'S SECRETS

By the 1960s, the Soviet system had fallen out of favor with Americans. Many American and British spies who were once willing to pass secrets to the Soviet KGB because of their communist beliefs were in short supply. Prospective spies still wanted to work for the KGB, but now they were in it for the money.

John Anthony Walker was a U.S. Navy communications specialist, able to access secret messages from nuclear scientists, military orders to naval fleets, and naval intelligence reports. His brother and son were also in the Navy. Walker had no sympathy for communism, but when his business venture failed in 1967, he became desperate for money. Walker headed to the Soviet Embassy in Washington, D.C., and offered the Russians classified information in exchange for several thousand dollars.

Soon Walker was on the KGB payroll. He was given a miniature camera for photographing documents and instructions for a dead drop outside the city. Walker was then able to leave documents and pick up cash without ever meeting another agent. By 1968, he was earning

Below: *Ethel and Julius Rosenberg are transported from court to prison after being found guilty of treason in 1951.*

Above: *The careers of John Anthony Walker and Aldrich Ames (1941–) began at the Soviet Embassy in Washington, D.C.*

$4,000 a month from his spying activities. He soon realized he could be making even more money if he had his own spy ring. He recruited a colleague named Jerry Whitworth. The pair passed top-secret information to the Soviets until the mid-1970s, when Whitworth backed out and Walker retired. Walker then recruited his brother Arthur and son Michael into the ring. Walker continued making monthly dead drops on Arthur's and Michael's behalf until 1985, when his disgruntled ex-wife tipped off the FBI. Walker and the other members of the spy ring were arrested, and all but Michael received life sentences. In his 18 years of spying, Walker helped the Soviets read more than 200,000 encrypted messages. As a result, the U.S. military had to rebuild their entire communications network, which cost $1 billion.

ALDRICH AMES

A year after Walker's arrest, bankrupted CIA agent Aldrich Ames walked into the Soviet Embassy in Washington, D.C., and offered to sell U.S. secrets. Ames revealed the identities of U.S. agents in the Soviet Union. After Ames became a Soviet spy, some of the CIA's Russian double agents were assassinated. Then, FBI agents began disappearing, too. An investigation began. When Ames came under suspicion, he twice passed lie detector tests. The investigation continued until 1990, when a KGB defector provided clues that pointed directly to Ames. He was immediately put under surveillance. When officers searched Ames's house, they found copies of reports he had written for the KGB, as well as proof that he had been paid for those reports. Because of Ames, at least 10 U.S. agents were assassinated. At least 100 intelligence operations were also ruined. Ames received more than $4 million from the KGB for the information, the most money a spy had ever earned. Ames was arrested in 1994 and sentenced to life in prison.

AN IDEAL SPY

At the same time the United States lost secrets via spies such as Walker and Ames, it also gained Soviet secrets. The most important of those secrets came from Dmitri Polyakov of the Soviet Military Intelligence organization, GRU. Polyakov was a Russian patriot, but he was disillusioned with the inequality and corruption in Soviet society. He wanted to give the United States an advantage in the Cold War.

Left: *John Walker (left) is escorted by a law enforcement officer on his way to court to appear on espionage charges. He is currently serving a life sentence in U.S. prison.*

Around 1961, while working undercover as a diplomat in New York, Polyakov approached FBI officers who assigned him the code name "Top Hat." For the next 25 years he worked as a U.S. double agent while steadily gaining access to valuable information. At that time, Polyakov accepted only gifts for his spying activites, such as fishing gear and power tools. The first intelligence Polyakov gave the FBI was the names of four U.S. soldiers and a British researcher who sold military secrets to the Soviet Union. Later, in 1972, Polyakov became head of the GRU's China section. He

Above: *This is the logo of the GRU—the intelligence agency of the Russian Federation.*

obtained documents tracking the breakdown in the relationship between the Soviet Union and China. That understanding of the rivalry between the two communist powers persuaded U.S. President Richard M. Nixon that it would be in the United States' best interest to improve its relations with China.

FROM HERO TO TRAITOR

Polyakov had several ways to make dead drops secure. When photographing documents, he sometimes used a type of film that could be developed only with special chemicals unknown to most people. Polyakov put the film inside fake hollow stones, which he left at sites in rural areas for his handlers. In 1974, Polyakov became a general. He was then able to provide his handlers with an increasing

Left: *Aldrich Ames left court after being convicted of espionage in 1994. He received a life sentence.*

JULY 1969
The United States wins the space race when *Apollo 11* lands on the Moon.

FEBRUARY 1972
U.S. President Richard M. Nixon meets Communist Chairman Mao Zedong in China beginning diplomatic relations between the United States and China, the Soviet Union's communist rival.

JULY 1975
The *Apollo-Soyuz* Test Project sends Soviet cosmonauts and American astronauts to space.

AUGUST 1979
U.S.S.R. invades Afghanistan to support its communist regime.

MARCH 1980
U.S. boycotts the Moscow Summer Olympics to protest the invasion of Afghanistan.

JUNE 1987
Soviet premier Mikhail Gorbachev announces *perestroika* and *glasnost*—policies aimed at openness and reform.

Right: *Crowds of Germans gather at Brandenburg Gate on November 10, 1989, just after the fall of the Berlin Wall.*

Below: *General Dmitri Polyakov (1921–1988) supplied information to the United States for 25 years. He was betrayed by both Aldrich Ames and Robert Hanssen and executed by the Soviets in 1988.*

number of U.S. military secrets. To increase security, the CIA designed an ingenious method of communication. Polyakov typed into a handheld device that automatically encrypted text. Next, he took an ordinary public bus. As the bus passed the U.S. Embassy, Polyakov pressed a button on the device that transmitted the information to a receiver inside the embassy. After Polyakov's retirement in 1980, he disappeared. Around 1990, the CIA discovered that Aldrich Ames had sold Polyakov's identity to the KGB. It is likely that he received the punishment reserved for Soviet traitors—a bullet in the back of the head and burial in an unmarked grave.

COLD WAR TENSIONS MOUNT

Increasing awareness of Soviet espionage contined to trouble the United States. In keeping with that distrust, the CIA began reconnaissance flights over the Soviet Union in 1955. One of its main recruits for those missions was Gary Powers. A member of the United States Air Force (USAF), Powers's exceptional abilities as a pilot made him an excellent choice to fly covert operations over enemy territory. In 1956, he joined the CIA U–2 program. The U–2 was a spy plane that could reach altitudes of 80,000 feet, allowing it to take aerial photographs of Soviet targets.

Although the incident remains a mystery, historians believe that Powers was shot down over the Russian city of Sverdlovsk (Ekaterinaburg) on May 1, 1960. Powers was unable to self-destruct the plane, and it landed intact—giving the Soviets proof that the United States had

FILM EXCERPT   GOVERNMENT DOCUMENT   INTERVIEW/BOOK EXTRACT   SONG EXCERPT

Above: *The headquarters of the KGB in Moscow, Russian Federation, housed the notorious Lubyanka prison, where Soviet dissidents were tortured and executed. It is now used by the FSB—the Russian FBI.*

TIME LINE
1988–1989

FEBRUARY 1988
Mordecai Vanunu is sentenced to 18 years in prison for treason and espionage after revealing Israel's nuclear program to the British press.

DECEMBER 1991
The U.S.S.R. is dissolved. Its republics become independent nations, ending the Cold War.

NOVEMBER 1989
The Berlin Wall dividing East and West Berlin is broken, paving the way for German reunification.

been spying on them. After being held for several months, Powers confessed. He was sentenced to 10 years in prison. However, after serving just 21 months, Powers was swapped for Soviet spy Vilyam Fisher (Rudolf Abel). He returned to the United States amid hostility. Some U.S. citizens felt he had betrayed the United States.

Cleared by a U.S. Senate Committee of any wrongdoing, Powers continued flying, but only for private companies. He was killed in 1977 in a helicopter crash in California. Powers was posthumously awarded the Prisoner of War Medal and National Defense Service Medal in 2000.

Below: *Ex-KGB officer Vladimir Putin (1952–), once president of the Russian Federation, is now Russia's prime minister.*

Left: *Gary Powers, one of the most famous figures in the Cold War, was killed in a helicopter crash in California on August 1, 1977.*

Above: One of many U.S. World War II propaganda posters warning the public of the need for secrecy.

During *World War II, posters warned of enemy spies. With the war's end, the heroic exploits of the shadow army became known and were celebrated on film. Espionage literature introduced a new, morally divided spy, and in the 1960s, spy stories even became comedic. Today, spies are a regular part of popular culture. Besides films and books, museums, board and digital games, and children's toys are based on spies and their gadgets.*

PROPAGANDA AND SPIES

World War II governments set up propaganda departments to warn people about enemy spies. Well-known illustrators were commissioned to produce posters advising people not to talk. In the United States, citizens were told that "loose lips sink ships" and to "keep it under your Stetson." In 1942, the message found its way into Britain's *The Next of Kin*, a film in which Nazi spies uncover plans to attack German territory. People were made aware of enemy spies, but they knew nothing of the real espionage operations carried out by their own governments.

WORLD WAR II STORIES

After the war, the spies' stories could finally be told, and they were irresistible material for filmmakers. Many stories did not need any exaggerations, and the films were made in a documentary style. The war had barely ended when the story of FBI double agent William Sebold appeared as *The House on 92nd Street*. Real FBI agents played themselves, and FBI head J. Edgar Hoover appeared in an introduction.

Similarly, in a film about a female spy, *Odette*, the head of the SOE, Maurice Buckmaster, appeared as himself. The World War II code breakers would not be revealed in fiction for a very long time, however. For

Left: *Scottish actor Sean Connery was the star of seven James Bond films between 1962 and 1983.*

"[Who] do you think spies are? Moral philosophers measuring everything they do against the word of God or Karl Marx? They're not! They're just a bunch . . . like me: little men, drunkards, . . . hen-pecked husbands, civil servants playing cowboys and Indians to brighten their rotten little lives."

Excerpt from the film script The Spy Who Came in from the Cold, an espionage thriller written by John Le Carré

Above: *The 2001 film* Enigma *was based on a novel by Robert Harris which told the true story of breaking the Enigma code.*

"It was part of his profession to kill people. He had never liked doing it and when he had to kill he did it as well as he knew how…. As a secret agent who held the rare Double-O prefix—the license to kill in the Secret Service—it was his duty to be as cool about death as a surgeon. If it happened, it happened. Regret was unprofessional…"

Excerpt from the espionage novel
***Goldfinger** by Ian Fleming*

DECEMBER 1998
Leo Marks, former head of SOE Communications, publishes his memoirs.

MARCH 2000
Ex-KGB officer Vladimir Putin becomes president of the Russian Federation.

SEPTEMBER 2000
Ex-MI5 officer David Shayler is charged with breaking Britain's Official Secrets Act.

SEPTEMBER 2001
The film *Enigma* tells a fictionalized story of the Bletchley Park code breakers.

SEPTEMBER 11, 2001
Attacks on the World Trade Center and the Pentagon create a new target for international espionage.

example, Bletchley Park employees were forbidden from talking about their work until 1975, in case their efforts were needed again. Once that silence ended, their accounts, like those of other wartime spies, first appeared as real-life histories, and then as fictionalized stories.

COLD WAR SPIES IN FICTION

Espionage was the most important weapon of the Cold War. As knowledge of spying increased, spy stories multiplied, too. The novels of ex-spies Graham Greene and John Le Carré, explored the moral dilemmas that spies faced. The stories posed the question of whether it was possible for a spy to be a moral person. The world had become more complex. During World War II, Nazi Germany, Japan, and their allies were clearly brutal. By the end of the Cold War, simple good versus evil stories seemed old-fashioned. Still, they lived on in James Bond action stories.

Above: *Postage stamps from 2008 featured the covers of Ian Fleming's* From Russia with Love *novel.*

> "I can tell you the license plate numbers of all six cars outside. I can tell you that our waitress is left-handed and the guy sitting up at the counter weighs 215 pounds and knows how to handle himself.
> I know the best place to look for a gun is in the cab of the gray truck outside, and at this altitude, I can run flat out for a half mile before my hands start shaking. Now why would I know that? How can I know that and not know who I am?"
>
> **Matt Damon's character Jason Bourne in the movie The Bourne Identity**

In the 1950s and 1960s, ex–Naval Intelligence Officer Ian Fleming wrote 12 novels and two books of short stories featuring British spy James Bond. The Bond character had many Cold War enemies, many of whom were Soviet agents. Although Bond is certainly luckier than any real-life spy, many elements of his world are true to life. Author Fleming used his own experiences as a spy to write the novels. The types of gadgets Bond uses—as well as the chain of command in British Intelligence, Bond's relationship with the CIA, and the use of codes for transmitting secret information—are factual. That mixture of fantasy and fact was a winning combination, making Fleming a bestselling author. His James Bond character starred in more than 20 films.

Above: *John Le Carré's 1974 novel,* Tinker Tailor Soldier Spy, *told the story of the Cambridge Five spy ring, with its main character based on Kim Philby.*

SPIES IN MUSEUMS AND MEDIA

Today, espionage is more popular than ever, especially among young people. The act of spying is even represented in museums. Washington, D.C., is home to an International Spy Museum. A huge range of mock spy gadgets, from invisible ink to wireless tracking systems, is available as children's toys.

Right: *A scene from the film* Mission: Impossible *shows Tom Cruise breaking into a high-security room within the CIA to steal a list of the identities of its undercover agents.*

 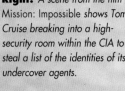

Spy films are also big business. In the film *Spy Kids,* the World War II organization OSS (Office of Strategic Services) reappears, but in the story it also employs children.

Uniting two of Hollywood's biggest stars—Brad Pitt and Angelina Jolie—*Mr. and Mrs. Smith* was a box-office hit. The film depicts a married couple, both of whom are spies, who are unaware of the other's secret life. After discovering they are working for rival agencies, they find themselves pitted against one another for survival.

Above: *The film* Windtalkers *tells the story of the Navajo code talkers.*

Another successful spy drama, *Mission: Impossible*, was originally a popular television series that aired between the 1960s and 1980s. *Mission: Impossible* made the move to the big screen in 1996, followed by three sequels. The films featured a team of highly skilled secret agents, the Impossible Missions Force (IMF). In each film, they used high-tech gadgets and disguises to carry out their missions. In the end, the disguises were always removed to reveal a member of the IMF team.

Windtalkers is an action film about the Navajo code talkers in the U.S. military during World War II. The film is set around the battle for Saipan. It starred Nicolas Cage and Christian Slater. Although the film was popular with fans, it drew criticism for focusing on the U.S. soldiers assigned to protect the Navajos, rather than on the code talkers themselves.

Could You Be a Spy?

Operation Spy at the International Spy Museum [is] a live-action spy adventure. You don't read about spies. You ARE the spy. You have one hour to locate a missing nuclear trigger before it ends up in the wrong hands. This is not an exhibit, it's as close to the real thing as you can get. Move quickly and think fast. Conduct surveillance. Polygraph a suspect agent. Steal secrets. Ready?

Advertisement for Operation Spy, at the International Spy Museum in Washington, D.C.

TIME LINE 2002–2007

JULY 2002
The International Spy Museum opens in Washington, D.C.

AUGUST 2002
Navajo code talkers are depicted in the film *Windtalkers.*

NOVEMBER 2006
Former KGB officer Alexander Litvinenko is assassinated with radioactive material in London.

JUNE 2007
A U.S. counterintelligence expert claims that Russian espionage efforts against the United States are "back at Cold War levels."

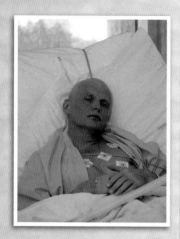

Above: *Former KGB agent Alexander Litvinenko lived in London as a political refugee. Since leaving the KGB, he feared for his life. In 2006, Litvinenko fell ill. It is believed that he was poisoned by a cup of tea contaminated with polonium-210, a radioactive substance. Litvinenko claimed that former KGB agents, directed by the Russian government, were responsible. He died on November 23, 2006.*

Below: *Robert Hanssen is arrested after making his final dead drop.*

In 1991, the Union of Soviet Socialist Republics (U.S.S.R.) was dissolved, ending the Cold War. A nation of 16 republics once collected into a single communist nation was now a group of independent countries. Most of them aspired to be democratic. The largest of those former republics was Russia. Despite the new, democratically elected government in Russia, however, the United States and the Russian Federation continued to spy on one another.

OLD HOSTILITIES CONTINUE

The world of espionage has undergone significant changes. A new type of spy called a whistleblower is on the scene. Economic spies help their countries compete with other nations for greater wealth. The computer revolution makes spying easier, allowing frightening new possibilities.

The man chosen to run Russia's post–Cold War spy program, Sergei Tretyakov, was himself working for the FBI. In 2000, he defected to the United States and resettled with his family in a secret location under a new name. In 2001, a senior FBI agent, Robert Hanssen, was arrested for spying for the KGB, then its successor, the SVR. The end of communism appears to have made little difference to the level of espionage between the Soviet Union and the United States. The motives of the spies also remained the same and usually involved dissatisfaction with their government and the lure of fast money.

WHISTLEBLOWER OR SPY?

A whistleblower is someone who reveals a secret to the press because he or she believes it should be out in the open. Political whistleblowers are usually treated as spies by the country whose secrets they have exposed. One of the most important whistleblowers was an Israeli, Mordechai Vanunu. In the 1980s, Israel publicly denied it was building nuclear weapons but, as an engineer at the country's Nuclear Research Center, Vanunu knew otherwise. He believed it was in the best interests of peace in the Middle East for the world

WILHELM CANARIS (1887–1945)

Wilhelm Canaris was leader of Abwehr, the German Intelligence group, from 1935 to 1944. He first supported Hitler, but after witnessing a series of Nazi atrocities, he began to secretly work against the Nazis. Canaris advised Spain's fascist leader, General Francisco Franco, not to allow Nazi troops into Spain. Canaris also tried to stop the Nazi invasion of Czechoslovakia, and attempted to negotiate peace with Allied powers. Canaris personally saved hundreds of Jews from concentration camps by pretending they were Abwehr spies. After a plot to assassinate Hitler failed, Canaris's secret double life was discovered. As punishment for his crimes against the Germans, he was hanged at a concentration camp just two weeks before it was liberated by the Allies.

IAN FLEMING (1908–1964)

Ian Fleming was raised as a member of the British upper class. During World War II, he was recruited into the British Naval intelligence unit under the code name 17F. Fleming became head of a successful intelligence-gathering outfit called 30 Assault Unit. Its members, trained in lock picking, safecracking, and unarmed combat, went into enemy territory to steal items such as code books and radio and radar equipment. After the war, Fleming used his experiences in espionage to create a fictional spy character, James Bond. Fleming's 12 novels were turned into popular films, making James Bond and his code name, 007, instantly popular all over the world.

PEARL CORNIOLEY (1914–2008)

Pearl Cornioley joined the British Special Operations Executive (SOE) in 1943. After seven weeks in combat and sabotage training, she was dropped by parachute into German-occupied France. She worked as a courier for a resistance network until its leader was captured. Cornioley then became a leader of another network and took charge of 1,500 resistance fighters. Under her leadership, the fighters carried out acts of sabotage against the Nazis, such as blowing up railway lines to prevent troops from reaching the battlefields. Cornioley was so successful that Germany offered one million francs for her capture. In spite of the Germans' desire to capture her, she survived the war and married a French resistance fighter.

ALLEN DULLES (1893–1969)

Allen Dulles is best known for being director of the CIA from 1953 to 1961. In his early life, during World War II, he ran a successful spy ring against the Nazis. Dulles entered diplomatic service at age 23 and worked in Austria, Switzerland, and Germany, partly as an intelligence gatherer. In 1942, Dulles became chief of the Berne station of the Office of Strategic Services—in charge of recruiting spies in Switzerland and gathering intelligence from them. His network of spies included Abwehr double agents. From them he was often able to report on the activities of the German resistance. His most valuable recruit was diplomat Fritz Kolbe, who supplied thousands of secret Nazi documents.

KIM PHILBY (1912–1986)

Kim Philby was a high-ranking British Intelligence officer, as well as a Soviet double agent. He was a member of a spy ring called the Cambridge Five—because each member attended Cambridge University where they became communists. The other members the group were Guy Burgess, Donald Maclean, Anthony Blunt, and John Cairncross. Philby expressed pro-Nazi views as a way of masking his communist sympathies. In 1944, he became head of counterespionage activities against the Soviets. It was a perfect position for protecting himself, but Philby still attracted suspicion. In 1963 he defected from Britain to the Soviet Union. Later he published his autobiography, *My Silent War*. Philby was responsible for the deaths of hundreds of British agents.

ANTHONY BLUNT (1907–1983)

Anthony Blunt was the most senior member of the Cambridge Five. He helped to recruit Anthony Burgess and Donald Maclean. During World War II he worked for MI5, and was able to pass on Ultra intelligence from intercepted Enigma messages to the Soviet Union. After the war he became a successful art historian and was appointed Surveyor of the Queen's Pictures—in charge of the royal family's art collection. Blunt even received a knighthood, making him Sir Anthony Blunt. In 1963, MI5 discovered his espionage, but it was kept secret until 1979. After that, Blunt was stripped of his royal title, but he was never brought to trial for spying.

ELIZABETH BENTLEY (1908–1963)

Born in Connecticut, Elizabeth Bentley studied in Florence, Italy, where she became interested in fascism. She soon changed allegiances and in 1935 she joined the Communist Party of the United States (CPUSAs). In New York, she became a courier for a Soviet agent, Jacob Golos, taking documents and messages from his network of American spies. When Golos suddenly died, Bentley took over the network. But in 1945, as she was about to be unmasked, Bentley approached the FBI and offered to become an informer. She gave the FBI the names of more than 100 Soviet spies, among them Julius and Ethel Rosenberg.

OLEG PENKOVSKY (1919–1963)

A colonel in the Soviet military intelligence organization the GRU, Oleg Penkovsky was also a double agent known to his handlers by the code name Agent Hero. In 1961 Penkovsky began passing important MI6 and CIA documents about Soviet weapons development. His Moscow contact was a female British spy, Janet Chisholm—the mother of three young children. Penkovsky would meet Chisholm in a local Moscow park and pass her documents and photographs, which she would hide in her baby's stroller. In 1962 the KGB learned about Penkovsky's spying from one of its double agents. He was immediately arrested and was executed some months later.

JUAN PUJOL (1912–1988)

A World War II Spanish double agent, Juan Pujol is one of the few people to have received military decorations from both Britain and Germany. Around 1940, Pujol became a German spy by pretending to be living in Britain (he was actually in Portugal) and in control of a network of agents. Once he was trusted by Germany's Abwehr agency, he offered his services to British Intelligence. Soon Pujol was actually in Britain and operating as a double agent (codename "Garbo"). Pujol passed misinformation to the Nazis throughout the rest of the war, and he was instrumental in the plot to convince the Germans that the Normandy landings would take place elsewhere. After the war he moved to Venezuela.

Abwehr The German intelligence organization that existed from 1922 to 1944.

agent Another word for spy; may also be called secret agent, or intelligence officer.

Allied nations Those nations allied against the Axis powers, primarily Britain, the Soviet Union, and the United States.

Axis nations Germany, Italy, Japan, and other countries opposed to the Allied nations.

cipher Different from a code, a cipher is a group of letters or symbols that stand for other letters. The cipher message appears as a meaningless pattern to those who do not understand what the words or symbols mean.

cipher machine Electromechanical device for creating millions of different ciphers.

ciphertext Text that has been encrypted with a cipher machine, so that it appears meaningless.

classified Information that has been officially designated as confidential or secret.

code The substitution of certain words or numbers for different ones, which disguise the true contents of that message.

code name The name by which a spy is known to his or her handler and intelligence agency. If a spy works with more than one agency, they will have a number of different code names.

code talker Someone who can speak in code. In World War II, Navajo Marines acted as code talkers so that the Japanese would not be able to decipher the messages.

communism An economic and political system in which wealth is owned collectively by the people through the state.

counterespionage Activity that aims to prevent or work against enemy espionage.

counterintelligence Activity to prevent enemy intelligence agencies from gathering covert or secret information. Spies may be said to operate covertly when they are under cover.

cryptanalysis The science of decrypting text, also called code breaking.

dead drop A prearranged place to exchange secret information and payment for the information.

defect To desert one country for another. During the Cold War a number of Soviets defected to Western countries, and communist sympathizers defected to the U.S.S.R.

democracy A nation that operates under the idea that the people hold the power to rule their own country, either directly or through their elected representatives.

diplomat Someone appointed to represent his or her government abroad. Spies often operate under cover as diplomats.

diplomatic relations Negotiation between the diplomats of different countries. To share open diplomatic relations with a country is to make a friendly gesture.

dissidents People who express an outward disagreement with a government or its policies.

double agent A spy who is secretly working for the government he or she is spying on. Some double agents start off by working for their government's enemy, while others are persuaded or decide to, change their allegiance.

encode To convert a plaintext message into a coded one.

encrypt To convert plaintext to a code or cipher. Enigma was the name given to a German cipher machine used throughout World War II.

espionage The use of spies to obtain secret information.

guerrilla warfare The name given to sabotage, raids, and other acts of combat carried out by a small group against a formal army.

hackers People who use mathematical skills to break into protected computer networks.

handlers In espionage, nonprofessional spies who are responsible for collecting intelligence from other spies and transmitting it to the intelligence agency.

intelligence Secret information including the information gained from the interception and decryption of coded messages.

intelligence agency An organization devoted to the gathering of intelligence, such as the CIA.

intercept To capture a communications signal intended for a different destination. In World War II, coded messages sent by radio were intercepted with a receiver.

Iron Curtain Phrase coined by British Prime Minister Winston Churchill to describe the division between democratic and communist states taking shape in Europe after 1946.

Magic Name given to the intelligence gained from intercepting and decrypting Japanese Purple messages in World War II.

microfilm Photographic film that photographs documents as images that are reduced in size.

misinformation False information designed to mislead a rival or enemy.

Morse Code A system of dots and dashes that represent the letters of the alphabet, transmitted by telegraph.

Nazis A German political party led by Adolf Hitler that started World War II in an effort to dominate the rest of the world. Under its theories of German racial superiority, the Nazis persecuted and killed millions of Europeans, particularly Jews.

neutral In wartime this means taking no side. Switzerland was a neutral country in World War II.

open source intelligence Information from publicly available sources that is of interest to spies.

plaintext Ordinary text that is about to be encrypted.

Purple Name given to the cipher machine used by Japanese diplomats to encrypt their messages in World War II.

ration card A card that gave the bearer the right to buy goods. During World War II, most food was rationed, or distributed in limited amounts.

resistance A secret group working toward the overthrow of forces occupying their homeland.

sabotage Destruction of equipment to weaken an enemy.

satellite An object that orbits Earth and monitors events on the ground, transmitting information to various goverments.

superpower A nation that is superior in political and military power. During the Cold War, the United States and Soviet Union were the world's superpowers.

surveillance Observing or monitoring someone secretly, often using electronic equipment such as telephone taps.

Ultra Name given to the intelligence gained from intercepting and decrypting German Enigma messages in World War II.

undercover Using an assumed identity. Spies usually operate undercover.

vetted Checked on someone's history. Potential spies are often vetted by intelligence agencies.

walk-in A spy who volunteers his or her services to an intelligence agency, rather than one who is recruited.

Please visit our web site at: **www.garethstevens.com**.
For a free color catalog describing Gareth Stevens Publishing's list of high-quality books, call 1-800-542-2595 (USA) or 1-877-387-3178 (Canada).
Gareth Stevens Publishing's fax: 1-877-542-2596

Library of Congress Cataloging-in-Publication Data

Scott, Carey.
    Spies and code breakers : a primary source history / by Carey Scott.
       p. cm. — (In their own words)
    Includes bibliographical references and index.
    ISBN-10: 1-4339-0049-1
    ISBN-13: 978-1-4339-0049-5 (lib. bdg.)
    1. Spies—History—20th century—Juvenile literature.
2. Espionage—History—20th century—Juvenile literature. 3. World War, 1939-1945—Secret service—Juvenile literature. 4. Spies—History—20th century—Sources—Juvenile literature. 5. Espionage—History—20th century—Sources—Juvenile literature. 6. World War, 1939-1945—Secret service—Sources—Juvenile literature. I. Title.
    JF1525.I6S35   2008
    327.12009—dc22   2008046628

This North American edition first published in 2009 by
Gareth Stevens Publishing
A Weekly Reader® Company
1 Reader's Digest Road
Pleasantville, NY 10570-7000 USA

This U.S. edition copyright © 2009 by Gareth Stevens, Inc. Original edition copyright © 2008 ticktock Entertainment Ltd. First published in Great Britain in 2007 by ticktock Media Ltd., Unit 2, Orchard Business Centre, North Farm Road, Tunbridge Wells, Kent, TN2 3XF, U.K.

Gareth Stevens Executive Managing Editor: Lisa M. Herrington
Gareth Stevens Editor: Joann Jovinelly
Gareth Stevens Creative Director: Lisa Donovan
Gareth Stevens Designers: Giovanni Cipolla, Ken Crossland
Gareth Stevens Production Manager: Paul Bodley, Jr.
Gareth Stevens Publisher: Keith Garton

Photo credits: B=bottom; C=center; L=left; R=right; T=top
Stefano Archetti/Rex Features: 6T; Beretta/Sims/Rex Features: 4T; Bettmann/Corbis: 27T, 43TL; Buena Vista/RGA: 33T; Central Intelligence Agency: 4-5C; CNN via Getty Images: 36BL; Thomas Coex/AFP/Getty Images: 37B; Corbis: 11, 15B, 23T, 42TL; Matt Crypto/Wikimedia Commons: 16B; Geoff Dann © Dorling Kindersley, Courtesy of the Imperial War Museum, London: 9T; Geoff Dann © Dorling Kindersley, Courtesy of Lorraine Electronics Surveillance: 6B; History is a Hoot, Inc. www.historyisahoot.com: 40TR; Hulton Archive/Getty Images: 8-9; Bob Daugherty/AP/PA Photos: 28B; Lear21/Wikimedia Commons: 30T; Lewis Durham/Rex Features: 15T; Everett Collection/Rex Features: 17B, 27B; Jon Freeman/Rex Features: 22-23; Getty Images: OFCT, 36T; Hodder & Stoughton (Used with permission): 34T; Nils Jorgensen/Rex Features: 48; Keystone/Hulton Archive/Getty Images: 24B, 25B, 31BL; Keystone/Getty Images: 12T. Herbie Knott/Rex Features: 42B; Life Magazine/Life Magazine/Time & Life Pictures/Getty Images: 16T, 40TL; MGM/RGA: 35T; Darz Mol/ Wikimedia Commons: 29T; Harry Myers/Rex Features: 41TL; NASA: 38; National Archives, RG226: 10T; National Archives and Records Administration: 11C; Courtesy of the National Security Agency: 1, 19BL, 20T, 20-21, 21T, 22T, 40B; Navy Historical Center: 14TR; Pictorial Press Ltd./Alamy: 20B; Popperfoto/Getty Images: 13B, 19BL, 41TL, 42TR; Press Agency/Getty Images: 18T; Rex Features: 7B, 8T, 32B, 33B, 41B; Roger-Viollet/Rex Features: 13T; Mark Rucker/Transcendental Graphics, Getty Images: 11T; Dave Rudkin © Dorling Kindersley, Courtesy of the RAF Museum, Hendon: 5B; Dave Rudkin © Dorling Kindersley, Courtesy of the Royal Signals Museum, Blandford Camp, Dorset: 12B; Shutterstock: OFCB, 4-5, 5T, 6-7, 7T, 25T, 27T, 31T, 38T; Sipa Press/Rex Features: 4BL, 14TL, 24-25, 28T, 29B, 36-37, 39B; Stuzhin & Cheredintzev/Keystone/Hulton Archive/Getty Images: 43TR; Swim Ink 2, LLC/Corbis: 32T; Ticktock Media Archive: 24TL; Cherie A. Thurlby/U.S. Department of Defense: 31BR; Universal/Everett/Rex Features: 6-7C; UPPA/Photoshot: 34B; Wikimedia Commons: 18B, 43B.

Every effort has been made to trace the copyright holders. We apologize in advance for any unintentional ommissions. We would be pleased to insert the appropriate acknowledgments in any subsequent edition of this publication.

Printed in the United States of America

1 2 3 4 5 6 7 8 9 10 10 09 08